ARMY OF COMPASSION

THE VISION OF DR. RICHARD DRAKE 1945-2011

DR. RICHARD N. DRAKE

Phoenix University of Theology International

ARMY OF
COMPASSION

Published by
Phoenix University of Theology International
Box 86054
Phoenix, AZ 85080
email: PhoenixUTI@gmail.com

Cover design: Carrie Wachsmann, Win Wachsmann
Cover photo: Chicago Theological Seminary
Courtesy John Schiebel Creative Commons License

Printed in USA

TABLE OF CONTENTS

INTRODUCTION

Dr. Richard Drake, "Dick" to his close friends,passed away, peacefully in his sleep, at 7:10am on February 9, 2011. He had been diagnosed with an Aortic aneurysm in November 2010.

Richard was the visionary and Founder of Phoenix University of Theology, a 501(c)(3) Non-profit Christian University, incorporated in the state of Arizona, June 15, 2001. Richard had a passion for learning, he spent countless hours researching the history of education and the political policies and laws that effect Christian education and the Church.

Thankfully, a number of Richard's orientation presentations outlining the vision for Phoenix University of Theology had been recorded. After his death, the recordings were transcribed and used to produce this book, using Richard's own words, as much as possible.

I believe that throughout the words of *The Army of Compassion*, you will get a sense of Richard's heart, and realization that education goes well beyond the textbook and requires drawing on a much wider range of sources in the pursuit of knowledge.

History proves that teaching had forever been an edict of the church; this truth inspired Richard's vision to uniquely positioned the University to reclaiming the educational prerogatives of Ecclesiastical authority along with its biblical standards and measures.

Phoenix University of Theology International, continues Richard's vision and represents a revival of the classic Ecclesiastical University System, which takes into consideration competencies, proven performance skills and proficiencies.

- We recognize many environments as appropriate to learning, not just the classroom
- We acknowledge the range of learning resources is limitless
- We confirm credits for documented learning, regardless of how it is accomplished
- We acknowledge the value of "revelational enlightenment"

It is our mission to validate those who can boldly teach sound, consistent doctrine. The University provides, through evaluation of one's *lifelong learning* and the evidence of God working through their life and ministry, a way for gifted and qualified men and women to receive the credentials they deserve because of their self-motivated study and revelation education. We realized that it is your gifting, your faith, your presence, and your presentation of God's call and purpose in your life, that speaks of your level of education and validates your "letters" or degree.

May God continue to guide and gift you with all you need to fulfill your potential in Him.

We are looking forward to finish the race together, to the glory of God.

KAREN E. DRAKE, **DOM, TMD, D.Min**

FORWORD

Dick had a wonderful yet hard life here on earth. I was thinking about Dick's legacy, Dick's contribution, Dick's faith, Dick's prophetic and visionary nature, Dick's calling, Dick's passion and compassion, Dick's leadership and Dick's influence. All of these attributes defined Dick while here on earth. Like a rock that is thrown into a pond, Dick's ripples have touched the shores of our lives. He has touched us and we have grown.

Look around at his extended spiritual family; that's legacy. Look around at his leadership; that's influence. Look at his relationship with God; that's faith. Look at his contribution; an idea that turned into the Phoenix University of Theology International, a new "mind- skin" that created a new wineskin in the Christian post graduate education realm; that's innovation. That's what I call living. God created Dick Drake on the eighth day. When God created Dick, He said, "I'll never do that again!"

You always had an advocate with Dick and everyone was his family. He aimed you upward in order to propel you onward. He was God-conscience but he also was real. He was heavenly minded and earthly good. He wasn't afraid to follow Jesus wherever he felt Jesus was leading him and he did. He was firm but loving when what he considered was God's vision, God's purposes and God's destiny was being challenged. He lead people by inspiration but wasn't afraid of perspiration. His tenacious spirit was infectious. Dick was a great disciple as well as a great disciple builder. Dick celebrated ministry and then delegated ministry. He would never quit because he couldn't quit.

Yes, Dick Drake was and is a real transformational person. Life was not normal with Dick. He challenged what was considered successful and the norm. When you met Dick, you left higher than when you came. He believed an egg could fly… after it's transformed. Albert Einstein once said; "You can't solve your problems with the same level of thinking that you had when you created them." Dick understood that and was sent by God to find a remedy for that.

I would describe Dick by words like encourager, "empower-er", innovator, initiator, reformer, catalyst, visionary, leader. He was Biblically correct and spiritually accurate, a motivator and a believer in the potential of people born for such a time as this. He saw where you could be... not where you were. People who would never have a chance had a chance with Dick. He moved mountains of doubt and objections in order to make leaders out of followers, men out of boys, women out of girls, doctors out of dropouts, hope out of disappointment, winners out of losers, champions out of chumps, apostles out of ushers, and authors out of the illiterate.

He created a wineskin for those who were called and longed for ministry but were ignored or marginalized by the institutionalized church elite. He was equally at home with the poorest or richest person, the spiritual or the practical person, or the logical or the emotional person. Whether they were currently successful or unsuccessful, Dick had a wonderful plan for their lives that could propel them to new heights, new realms, and new dimensions. It takes an amazing person to do that. He has touched us, and in many cases changed us...and...that is all you can ask of anyone!

Dick lived the following principle. "We are not human beings going through a temporary spiritual experience. We are spiritual beings going through a temporary human experience." Dick understood that life this side of the curtain was temporal. He also understood that life on the other side of the curtain is eternal. He realized you don't follow Jesus because He makes life better. You follow Jesus because He is better than life and our encouragement for each today.

The opportunity to live is the greatest of all gifts. It means that God planned you from the beginning of the foundations of the earth. It means that your presence here on earth is not an accident. It means that you have been decreed, assigned and dedicated in advance for a particular purpose that only you can do while here on this earth. It means you are the way you are because of why you are. It means that you have the potential to enjoy the privileges and presence of God in heaven for all eternity. In other words, when the Lord made you too, He looked at you and said, "I'll never do that again!" From the moment you were born, God has been getting you ready for what He has ready for you! Now, go from here and complete in your life what God used Dick to start in your life. Think of it... God sent

Dick into our lives to start what was in our lives! Dick, by his life, is teaching us how to outlive our life. God is moving PUTI from a man to a movement. After all, that is what Jesus did with his disciples.

That is why the Psalmist wrote in Psalm 116:15, *"Precious in the sight of the Lord is the death of his godly ones."* You might be thinking what will happen to Karen, to me or to Phoenix University of Theology International.

God has not abandoned Karen, Dick's spiritual children or Phoenix University of Theology International. I can assure you, that allowing Dick's death was not a decision taken lightly by God. In this, He has made provision for Karen, for us and for PUTI. Why? God is good. Karen will get to see Dick again and we will too. This is not just wishful emotion based thinking of bereaved humans. This is based on the word of God. We are not like others who grieve but have no hope. Hope is the expectation of future good. Our hope is in the Lord as Dick's was too.

Let me finish with some scripture that reveals every persons God desired Rite of Passage. I'm reading from 1 Cor. 15:42-58. Listen to those last words in the Bible…. *"O Death, where is your victory? Oh death, where is your sting?"*

13

God planted the seed of a perishable body but through death came the harvest of an imperishable body. We are sown a natural body, but are raised in a spiritual body. If there is a natural body, there is also a spiritual body. The spiritual is not first, but the natural, then the spiritual. The first man is from earth, earthy; the second man (who is the same man) is from heaven. Life springs out of death. There is always a spring, summer, autumn, and winter…but then spring comes again. The four seasons are trying to tell us something, aren't they? They are saying seedtime and harvest time. I'd guess, from God's perspective, spring has sprung.

Dr. Ed Delph

NationStrategy

CHAPTER 1

WORDS AND REVELATION OF DR. RICHARD DRAKE

Phoenix University of Theology International is designed after the "classic" university system. A university in the classic sense is an association of teaching disciplines. Cities like Paris, France and Bologna, Italy, once were famous for their universities. Men who were taught in a given field gathered in these cities and the universities would teach whoever wanted to learn from them and in their subject; whether it was medicine, law, theology, etc. The university was formed through various teaching disciplines or colleges and the university association set the standards for awarding degrees. Men gathered from all over the world to listen to lectures. The teacher determined when a student knew sufficient information to be recommended to the university for a degree.

Classic universities were very competitive and they had little respect for each other. If you wanted to teach at the University in Paris, you had to earn a degree from the University of Paris. You couldn't come to the University of Paris with a degree from Bologna, Italy and expect to teach.

Unfortunately, today, man's lack of wisdom says, our universities have diversity. So today's "Universities" have instructors from all universities and all walks of life and all disciplines. So they confuse and confound the world so much, and they think they're smart and they're not.

Many Bible schools today are graduating young men and women year after year who know the theory of the Spirit-filled life but do not enjoy the experience. These men and women go out into today's churches and create a generation of Christians who "have never felt the power of the Holy Spirit."

1 Timothy 1:6-7 warns us, *6 But certain individuals have missed the mark on this very matter [and] have wandered away into vain arguments and discussions and purposeless talk. 7 They are ambitious to be doctors of the Law, but they have no understanding either of the words and terms they use or of the subjects about which*

they make dogmatic assertions. Thereby, they are undermining the faith of some.

Also addressed in, 2 Timothy 3: *But know this, that in the last days perilous times will come, 2 For men will be lovers of themselves, lovers of pleasure rather than lovers of God, 5 <u>having a form of godliness but denying its power</u> ... from such people turn away... 7 always learning and never able to come to the knowledge of the truth. 8 so do these also resist the truth: men of corrupt minds, disapproved concerning the faith.*

It is because of this lack of preparedness and understanding about the power and the presence of the Holy Spirit, that:

1. Fifteen hundred pastors leave the ministry each month due to moral failure, spiritual burnout or contention in their churches.
2. Four thousand new churches begin each year, but over seven thousand churches close.
3. Eighty percent of Seminary and Bible School graduates who enter the ministry will leave the ministry within the first five years.

4. Ninety percent of pastors said their seminary or Bible school training did only a fair to poor job preparing them for ministry.

5. Fifty percent of pastors' marriages will end in divorce.

6. Eighty percent of pastors and eighty-four percent of their spouses feel unqualified and discouraged in their role as pastors.

7. Fifty percent of pastors are so discouraged that they would leave the ministry if they could, but have no other way of making a living.

If you want to teach at Phoenix University of Theology, Inernational, you need a degree from here, because we want to know what you are going to be teaching.

IN THE FIELD, OR THE WORLD OF THE CHURCH, WE RECOGNIZE FIRST OF ALL THAT GOD IS OUR TEACHER.

We hear from God because we are called of God and we're taught by God. So, it doesn't make any difference if you have a degree from Harvard and you want to teach at Phoenix University of Theology International, you need a degree from here as well, because you need to know what we're all about.

Let me make the point about the term or the title, "Doctor." The first thing I want you to do is make an association between these terms, "doctor and doctrine." A Doctor is one who teaches sound doctrine.

The word Doctor which is, *didáskalos* in Greek, means: ("to teach") an instructor, one who imparts knowledge or skills, one acknowledged for their mastery in their field of learning, one competent in theology. The word *didáskalos* is translated in the New Testament three different ways. Some places it is translated **teacher**, some places it's translated **master,** and some places its translated **doctor.**

The title "Doctor" in the church was originally **"Doctor Ecclesia."** A father or a teacher of the church. The Doctor of Ecclesia did not go through a specific course curriculum. They were recognized by the resident wisdom in their heart and mind and the depth of their understanding and espousing and teaching of doctrine. They were "gifted" and recognized by the Ecclesiastical authority and that is how they received their degree.

In the following scripture references there are some uses of the term Doctor in the original Biblical translation where we use the word Teacher, today.

One example is where it is talking about the gifts: 1 Corinthians 12: 27 *Now ye are the body of Christ, and members in particular. 28 And God hath set some in the church, first apostles, secondarily prophets, thirdly teachers, after that, miracles, then gifts of healings, helps, governments, diversities of tongues. Today* **the scriptures read** *"that God set some pastors and teachers."*

The oldest translation uses the word Doctor, as opposed to Teacher. Another example is Luke 2:46, it says *"And it came to pass, that after three days they found him in the temple, sitting in the midst of the 'doctors', both hearing them, and asking them questions."*

It wasn't until the Middle Ages that churches in Paris and Italy allowed the use of the title Doctor to be associated 'with any degree' other than that of *Doctor Ecclesia,* no longer relating specifically to those that taught doctrine. One of the things that made it more appropriate, to use the title, was because in the Middle Ages if you were going to be an attorney or medical doctor you must also have studied theological doctrine. You could not have had a degree awarded if you did not have the foundation of and in the understanding of "The Word and the Doctrine of God."

In America, the Bible and the Christian faith were foundational in our educational and judicial system, unfortunately however in:

In 1947, there was a radical change of direction in the

Supreme Court when it banished the prayer:

"Almighty God, we acknowledge our dependence on Thee. We beg Thy blessings upon us and our parents and our teachers and our country. Amen."

In 1963, the Supreme Court ruled that Bible reading was outlawed as unconstitutional in the public school system. The court offered this justification: *"If portions of the New Testament were read without explanation, they could and have been psychologically harmful to children."*

Reading of the Bible, after 1963, was unconstitutional in the public school system though the Bible was quoted 94 percent of the time by those who wrote our constitution and shaped our nation and its system of education and justice and government.

In 1965, the Courts denied as unconstitutional the rights of a student in the public school cafeteria to bow his head and pray audibly for his food.

In 1980, The case of Stone vs. Graham outlawed the Ten Commandments in our public schools. The Supreme Court said this: *"If the posted copies of the Ten Commandments were to have any effect at all, it would be to induce school children to read them. And if they read them, meditated upon them, and perhaps venerated and observed them, this is not a permissible objective."* What?

Is it not a permissible objective to allow our children to follow the moral principles of the Ten Commandments? Today public schools have taken God and removed His Word as far away as possible from our education and our educational system.

This has gone on for too long. We as Christian leaders have allowed this to happen by passively allowing the world to dictate and impose their agenda. We have failed to fulfill our mandate to take "**dominion over the earth**" by boldly proclaiming His Word and bringing honor to our Maker.

Matthew 5:18-19 tells us: **18 *For truly I tell you, until the sky and earth pass away and perish, not one smallest letter nor one little hook will pass from the Law until all things are accomplished. 19 Whoever then breaks or does away with or relaxes one of the least [important] of these commandments and teaches men so, shall be called least [important] in the kingdom of heaven, but he who practices them and teaches others to do so shall be called great in the kingdom of heaven.***

We can look in our Bibles today and find that the word "Doctor" has been replaced in the revised versions. We keep abridging that word out more and more because in our society, in the United States in particularly, when we say doctor, we are generally referring to a "medical doctor", and we should be saying, my "medical doctor" or my "physician", because when you say "Doctor", you are talking about "your Instructor in Doctrine" who as your preacher, has earned that title by his gifting and ability to teach sound, consistent doctrine.

A primary reason for Phoenix University of Theology International is to again establish the association of the term "Doctor" with "instruction in sound doctrine." As a University of Theology, we are used of the Lord to find men and women, and to certify that these men and women are teaching sound, consistent, doctrine on the earth. We are warned in 2 Timothy 4: *3 For time shall be, when men will not endure sound doctrine; but after their own lusts shall they heap to themselves teachers, having itching ears, for something pleasing and gratifying, they will gather to themselves one teacher after another chosen to satisfy their own liking and to foster the errors they hold, 4 And will turn aside from hearing the truth and wander off into myths and man-made fictions.*

The Ph.D. is not offered at Phoenix University of Theology International. Ph.D. stands for Doctor of Philosophy, which is considered a secular degree.

Webster's dictionary defines philosophy as: "The disciplines presented in university curriculums of science and the liberal arts, **except medicine, law, and theology.** Philosophy is the investigation of questions about existence, knowledge, logic and ethics."

It includes:

Aesthetics - (the creation of beautiful or significant things; art)

Metaphysics - (the philosophical study of the nature of reality, concerned with such questions as the existence of God, the external world, etc.)

Epistemology - (the rational investigation of questions about existence and knowledge and ethics)

Every degree title or distinction from Phoenix University of Theology International must clearly indicate that it is a Christian ministry offering only "Theological Study" degrees and must not be confused with a Liberal Arts Education. All our degree programs are designed to improve the skills and success of those **committed to Christian ministry**.

We are confirming and validating those whom God sends that have received spiritual truths as Paul speaks of in: 1 Corinthians 2:2 *I did not come proclaiming to you the testimony of God in lofty words of eloquence or human philosophy and wisdom... 4 but they were in demonstration of the [Holy] Spirit and power. 5 So that your faith might not rest in the wisdom of men (human philosophy) but in the power of God. 6 We do impart a [higher] wisdom; but it is indeed not a wisdom of this present age or of this world nor of the leaders and rulers of this age, who are being brought to nothing and are doomed to pass away. 7 But rather what we are setting forth is a wisdom of God once hidden and now revealed to us by God. 8 None of the rulers of this age or world perceived and recognized and understood this... 10 Yet to us God has unveiled and revealed them by and through His Spirit... 12 Now we have not received the spirit [of] the world, but the [Holy] Spirit Who is from God. 13 And we are setting these truths forth in words not taught by human wisdom but taught by the [Holy] Spirit, combining and interpreting spiritual truths with spiritual language. 14 But the natural, non-spiritual man does not accept or welcome or admit into his heart the gifts and teachings and revelations of the Spirit of God, for they are folly (meaningless nonsense) to him; and he is incapable of knowing them because they are spiritually discerned and estimated and appreciated... 16 But we have the mind of Christ and do hold the thoughts (feelings and purposes) of His heart.*

CHAPTER 2

THE HISTORY OF PHOENIX UNIVERSITY OF THEOLOGY INTERNATIONAL

Early in 2001 Dr. Richard Drake licensed his tenth man from the street to preach. For 10 years he had been teaching men off the street, through the "Institute for Christian Maturity" and over that same period of time had licensed ten men.

Then God said to him, *"Now I'm sending you for the ten thousand."* Everyone who knew Dr. Drake (Richard) knew his story of how a simple childhood song, he learned in Sunday school, had become his motto; it expressed the spirit and pursuit of his life and ministry.

STOUT-HEARTED MEN

You who have dreams, if you act they will come true.

To turn your dreams to a fact, it's up to you.

If you have the soul and the spirit, never fear it; you'll

see it thru.

Hearts can inspire, other hearts with their fire,

For the strong obey when a strong man shows them the

way.

Refrain:

Give me some men, who are stout-hearted men,

Who will fight, for the right they adore.

Start me with ten, who are stout-hearted men,

And I'll soon give you ten thousand more.

Shoulder to shoulder and bolder and bolder,

They grow as they go to the fore.

Then there's nothing in the world can halt or mar a

plan,

When stout-hearted men can stick together man to man.

The first and only time Dr. Richard Drake met Dr. Edwin Louis Cole, the founder of Christian Men's Network (CMN) — Dr. Drake spoke to Dr. Cole of his vision for the "Army of Compassion" and his commitment to God.

That, if God would give him 10 men who were stout hearted men, He would soon give him 10,000 more. Immediately Dr. Cole and Dr. Drake broke into song and began marching in place, at this formal event with everyone in attendance watching inquisitively. Dr. Richard Drake and Dr. Edwin Louis Cole had been given the same marching orders, *"make disciples of all men."* Matthew 28:19

Jesus broke down the partition wall, and commissioned his disciples to go everywhere, and bring the "world" to the knowledge of himself.

It has been said that Phoenix University of Theology International is to the Army of Compassion (Army of God) what Annapolis is to the Navy (Naval Academy). In Navy terms, Dr. Richard Drake was the Captain or Officer in Charge and Karen (his wife) was his First Mate; the officer who ranks just below the Captain of the ship and would take over in the event that the Captain can no longer perform his duties.

The University, like Annapolis, gives students the teaching and professional training they need to become effective officers in the "Army of Compassion." Men and women that are responsible for the priceless lives of multiple-millions of hurting people worldwide.

This program helps the student develop a clear sense

of his own relationship with her Heavenly Father and the ability to articulate His Word and His message, clearly to others. The students, like those graduating from Annapolis are persons of integrity: "standing for that which is right" respecting human dignity, honesty and the welfare of others.

The Academic Program at Phoenix University of Theology International will begin with a core curriculum that includes courses in Christian Ethics, Servant Leadership, The Responsibility for the Church in the Community, Compliance and Accountability, My Brother's Keeper and Reconciliation. At the same time, our Majors Programs give the student the opportunity to develop a particular area of scholastic interest such as Chaplaincy, Marriage and Family Counseling, Healing and Impartation.

Our goal is to offer a broad-based Christian education to qualify the students for every area of Ministry. We don't just tell students about life in ministry; classroom studies are expected to account for only about one-third of the time spent learning. As a student, one is required to live what one learns through many hours of practical experience. A graduate from Phoenix University of Theology International is a living example of The Word of God and will reflect His compassion for mankind in thoughts, words and deeds.

Ron Hembree

When Dr. Drake arrived in Phoenix in 2001, he was not sure where he was supposed to go or what he was supposed to do; he only knew that God had told him that the "provision for the vision" was in Phoenix.

The first church Dr. Drake attended was Dr. William Hepfner's church, called *Power House*; the same name as the Rehab Ministry in Humboldt, Tennesee. Dr. Drake was invited to attend a prayer breakfast that was held each week. Upon arriving at the "Good Friends Prayer Breakfast", he found out that the minister hosting the prayer breakfast was Ron Hembree.

In the 1970's, Dr. Richard Drake had been the director of the Arkansas State Claims Commission where he had oversight of the insurance claims submitted by the prison system. During the same time Ron Hembree was a young Assemblies of God preacher who had gone to the Arkansas prison system and built the chapel at the Tucker and Cummings unit. The chapel is still in operation today. So, it was reunion time. Ron Hembree asked Dr. Drake to tell the group what he was doing in Phoenix. God had immediately given him acceptance, connection and involvement with ministries in the Phoenix area.

About the same time, the director of the White House office on "Community and Faith Based Initiatives" had resigned. The Governor of Tennessee, Don Sunquist, had been a friend of Dr. Richard Drake's for many years. Don called and asked if he could submit Richard's resume to the president for the job. Dr. Drake said he would not pursue the position, but if it pursued him he would accept. On September 11, 2001 (9/11), Dr. Drake was in Kentucky at a meeting of the Southern Governors Association with his friends Don Sunquist and Mike Huckabee, the governor of Arkansas, meeting with people from the White House, when the planes hit the Twin Towers. Shortly, after that event, the Lord spoke to him, saying: *"withdraw your name; Go back to Phoenix and build the 'Army of Compassion' from the ground up."*

Dean Radtke

Upon his return to Phoenix, Dean Landis introduced Dr. Drake to Dean Radtke. Dean Radtke was beginning a "CEO and Leadership Training", with Ron Hembree. Dean Radtke offered Ron Hembree a tuition-free leadership training that normally cost $1750. Ron Hembree said, "I think 'Dick' Drake is the man you need to see,"

So, Dean Landis and Dean Radtke came to hear about the Army of Compassion from Dr. Drake.

Dean Radtke asked, *"How can I help you?"*

Dr. Drake said, *"We need your teaching but we can't afford your fee. Most of my guys are poor including me."* So Dean Radtke partnered with the University to provide one million dollar's worth of free training to students of the University. He gave his first tuition-free CEO and Leadership Workshop in Mesa, Arizona in January of 2002. Dr. Dean Radtke was the first to receive his Doctoral Degree from the Phoenix Theological Seminary. Shortly after that Ron Hembree was awarded his Doctoral Degree as well.

We look for God to confirm our steps as we walk by faith with Him. And He will do that often enough, frequently enough to keep us headed in the right direction and to keep us energized and motivated so that we know we're on the right course. Countless times throughout our lives and ministries, we can see how God will put us in just the right place at just the right time and put those people that He wants to be a part of His work into our life when we need them; some for a lifetime, some for a season and some for only a moment in time.

God told Dr. Drake that He was going to send authors

to the University. The men and women who were writing the contemporary understanding of His message to this generation, and that through the "University" system, we would be able to put that information into the hands of multitudes of thousands of people around the world. If we wait for a textbook to come through the system and be approved to be taught at a seminary or in a classroom we wouldn't find the kind of material that God wants us to have; plain, simple and powerful. God has given us a way to reach multitudes of people using the proper words to express His revelation and *compassion* in an influential and effective way.

Douglas Layton

Douglas Layton was the third Doctoral graduate from Phoenix Theological Seminary. He has traveled extensively throughout 40 countries and has founded ministries in Afghanistan, Pakistan, India and Iraq. He has shared the Gospel with thousands of Muslims and authored numerous books on Islam, including *Answering Islam* and *Our Father's Kingdom.* These books share his hands-on experience and passion for the Lord. His mission is to protect and enable pastors, believers and churches in traditionally Islamic countries that long to impact their nations with the Gospel.

Ed Delph

The first book that God gave Dr. Drake a heart desire to encouraged to get published was a doctoral thesis entitled *Intelligent Fire*. It was presented by Ed Delph. Dr. Drake realized that this man had his same heart and vision because he had been listening to the same guy, his Father in Heaven. Ed had the same revelation that God had given Dr. Drake about what we needed to do to reposition the church in the community with power, respect and influence.

So Dr. Drake said, *"Ed, we've got to publish this as a book and we will use it as a text."* Ed Delph retitled his book *Church@Community*. Dr. Drake continued to call it *Intelligent Fire* because it sets people's heart and mind on fire to do the work of the Lord.

Dr. Delph is in a different country almost every month. He's teaching and preaching this principle all over the world. Everyone that learns from him can earn continuing education credit through Phoenix University of Theology International.

Dr. Delph explains that *"Teaching is one-way*

communication. Learning is two-way communicatins. Teaching is output based. Learning is outcome based. Teachers tend to think that it is their job to broadcast and the student's job to receive."

At Phoenix University of Theology International, we assign each student a personal Mentor, because we believe that, *it is the true Mentor that ensures the one being taught actually understands and applies what is being taught correctly. Formation is more important than information.*

When a student gets to the point that he not only knows and understands Dr. Delph's teaching; but, is himself teaching it, the student can receive even more University credits because, the more a student learns in a given subject and the more he can apply it, the more credit he can earn. The student promotes and sells Dr. Delph's books. They also promote the degree they received through Phoenix University of Theology International. As a student one puts their title on their material and identifies that one received their degree from Phoenix University of Theology International on all books, publications and resumes.

Through the University, we offer the instant dissemination of revelation to a group of men and women who can impact the nation and the world. So, when information comes through their student work and that work is approved by the University and it is a publication that we choose to endorse and to certify for credit, then it becomes at least an elective in each student's degree program.

Ultimately, we intend to have all of the degrees that are earned through this University, earned through curriculum that was produced through this University, by graduates from the University. The men and women writing the contemporary understanding of God's message to this generation and who have been approved through the University system, will ultimately be able to put that information into the hands of multitudes of thousands of people around the world.

If we had to wait for a textbook to come through the system and be approved to be taught at a seminary or in a classroom we wouldn't find the kind of material that God wants us to have; plain, simple and powerful. God has given us a way to reach multitudes of people using the proper words to express His revelation and *compassion* in an influential and effective way. That is our strategic plan for growth. The Lord said *"The provision for the vision is in Phoenix."*

When God sent Dr. Drake to Arizona it was in search of "ten thousand" men and women to build an Army of Compassion that would turn the world to Christ in this generation by the dissemination of His love and His power through His charity, *or love* and His message.

John Binkley

When John Binkley sent his work in as partial requirement for his doctoral degree, the original title was *Wealth and Riches*. Dr. Drake said he thought it sounded like prosperity preaching, one of those "name it and claim it" guys. After reading the book, he said, "*It is not about wealth and riches at all, it's about the Dominion Commission that God had put in his heart. This fellow's got my revelation.*"

John Binkley now calls his book, *A Place Called Destiny*. His book is certified by the Accrediting Association for Theological Studies, (AATS), as recommended curriculum for anyone seeking a Market Place Ministry Degree. God has brought men and women to the University that have been given revelation. They put these revelations into writing and we can now use these writings as text to teach whomever God sends to this University. What a wonderful God we serve. How easy He makes life look. How smart He will make you look if you let him.

In February of 2003 Phoenix Theological Seminary held a CEO and Leadership Training workshop with Dr. Dean Radtke and concluded the event with our first formal Graduation. This first graduating class included authors such as Dr. Terry Crist, *Learning the Language of Babylon* and *Image Maker*, Dr. Wellington Boone, *My Journey with God* and *Low Roads to New Heights*, Dr. Ed Delph, *Church@Community* and Dr. Keith Rushing. Other Ministry and Church leaders graduating included: **Dr. Dean and Kay Landis, Dr. Lee and Jan Melby, Dr. Tom Ryan, Dr. Gene Gallant, Dr. Roger and Judy Keller, Dr. Steve Phinney, Minister Mark Creighton, Tim Oergel** and **Hugh Tedesk**i.

In addition, other notable alumni include **Dr. Ben Kinchlow** - an evangelist best known for being co-host of The 700 Club from 1975 to 1988 and again from 1992 to 1996. He also hosted other shows on the Christian Broadcasting Network such as Straight Talk and a radio talk show, Taking It To The Streets.

Dr. Leo Godzich - (April 30, 1969 – October 28, 2011) is an alumnus. The author of numerous books and training materials, including *Is God in Your Marriage.* Leo founded the National Association of Marriage Enhancement (N.A.M.E.) a ministry to promote marriage and to train and certify lay marriage counselors. There are now over 200 NAME centers across the globe on six different continents.

Dr. T. L. Osborn - (December 23, 1923 – February 14, 2013) another alumnus, was an American Pentecostal evangelist and author based in Tulsa, Oklahoma. Osborn's crusades in Thailand in 1956 and Uganda in 1957 are said to have laid the foundations for substantial growth in Pentecostalism in those countries. Osborn authored several books, including: *Healing The Sick, Soulwinning, God's Love Plan, The Good Life,* and *The Message That Works.*

Thomas Dexter "T. D." Jakes, Sr. is the bishop/chief pastor of The Potter's House, a nondenominational American megachurch, with 30,000 members, located in Dallas, Texas is a graduate. Other aspects of Jakes' ministry include an annual revival called "MegaFest" that draws more than 100,000 people, an annual women's conference called "*Woman Thou Art Loosed.*"

Luke Barnett – son of Pastor Tommy Barnett and Lead Pastor of Phoenix First. Pastor Luke's vision focuses on family, community, and social compassion program development. With his direction, Phoenix First Church has developed The Rescue Project at the Phoenix Dream Center, a Food Bank and many other social programs.

Edwin Louis Cole (September 10, 1922 - August 27, 2002) also known as Ed Cole, was the founder of the Christian Men's Network, a religious organization devoted to helping Christian men and fathers. He published many books, ministered on Christian Television Networks, established a radio ministry and evangelized worldwide.

The university's job is not just some sort of objective assessment of written material. It is the discernment and assessment of the individuals that God is sending and what they have in them that reflects Him. Our strategy is to harvest, not recruit. Students are here because they were encouraged by what they heard about the University or they were recommended by someone who knew about the University and its vision and perceived they are the kind of person that God would confirm here.

Harvard doesn't produce business geniuses, it recruits them. MIT doesn't produce technological genii, it recruits them.

We do not produce great Theologians, God does; and then He sends them to us, we recognize them and then we get credit for being part of their life and ministry. **Makes us look smart**!

We have thousands of people from all over the world right now studying curriculum that the University recognizes for credit. So, a student is in class and they don't even know it.

Part of the strategy that we have for growth and recognition is - recognizing how many gifted men and women we have teaching the Word of God from a pulpit every Sunday morning? The most gifted teachers in the world, are busy in the church.

A lot of these "Sunday Morning Preachers" have what they call a Bible College degree or training. They call it that because the teacher knows the level and depth of what they are teaching is at the College Level and they want their congregation to know that too. But, unfortunately, with the world trying to gain a grip on education and accreditation it makes it difficult if not impossible to take what you learn at "Bible College" to any other college.

The information is great- you learned it and you know it. But, essentially you couldn't go anywhere with that knowledge, until now. The Lord has given us a system at Phoenix University of Theology International, which we call "**Sunday University**" to get that curriculum accredited through the Accrediting Association and certified for value. If that preacher has a degree through Phoenix University of Theology International, he can get his curriculum accredited and then becomes a certified teaching alliance, teaching at the college level. Then, anyone that learns under that certified teacher can take their "Certificate of Completion" and include it in their MAP-PAC, so we can add it to their Phoenix University of Theology International transcript and they have a developing transcript that the student can keep from now on.

The Institute for Christian Maturity was started by Dr. Drake as a teaching vehicle, to teach people based not on their gender or on their age but on the level of maturity they had in Christ and with the Word. He taught on a semester basis so the students could continue to take progressively more in-depth studies. It was leading with a specific learning objective and it gave Dr. Drake the discipline to know that he was leading his disciples, or flock in a way that matured them in their faith and relationship with Christ and he wasn't just talking about an interesting topic or a Bible story on Sunday morning.

When God started sending Dr. Richard Drake the men off the street, many of them didn't know the Word of God. They didn't have drivers' licenses or even a high school diploma. So, he used the Institute as a vehicle to teach them because they didn't qualify for seminary entrance. Until he could get them to that level of Biblical understanding, he couldn't put them in the Seminary without lowering the standards of the Seminary. But they were "on fire for God." The men wanted to know the Word and he couldn't give it to them fast enough. He taught everyday, weeks after weeks and they just ate it up and ate it up. Pretty soon the men were teaching each other, they were "on fire for God." They were hungry for the Word and many of the men wanted to go on to Seminary. Some went on and are now themselves preaching in their own churches.

The ten men that Dr. Drake taught in Tennessee were men that were the least of the least; the last of the lost, they were drug addicts. The tenth guy was dying of aids that he'd gotten from intravenous drug use. He decided to give his life to the Lord and came to Dr. Drake's church. He'd heard about his ministry, he was afraid of him, but where else could he go? He was dying. So he thought he would try out Jesus.

On Brent's first night at the Good Samaritan Center, the Lord told Dr. Drake to take some water to the service; he was going to be baptizing someone. The Lord had Dr. Drake dip his fingers into the water and he flicked the water into Brent's face three times as he said:

"In the name of the Father
·and of the Son
·and of the Holy Spirit. "

As soon as Dr. Drake finished speaking, Brent ran to the restroom because he said the water, when it hit his face, burned so hard he wanted to go and see how many burn marks he had on his face. God burned the sin and the aids out of this boy's life. And healed him miraculously and Dr. Drake didn't even know that he was sick.

After licensing his 10th man, God told Dr. Drake, because he had been faithful to teach whomever He had sent, God was sending him for the "ten thousand men" and they were going to be the best of the best and Dr. Drake could pick them. So God was going to give him the best of the best to serve Him and His work through the "Army of Compassion."

As a student you get to put your name on that list. Phoenix University of Theology International is harvesting a group of people that God has empowered and gifted to be used in this hour to build a conquering army and take dominion in the earth.

Charles King

Dr. Richard Drake's proudest accomplishment in being used of the Lord was a young black fellow named Charles King. Charles King was stumbling about a hundred yards, going to his sister's purse to retrieve a gun. He wanted to kill two guys he had just seen at the pool hall that had attacked him the night before and had stolen his car.

Dr. Drake had felt led that Sunday night to go to a place called The Crossing, which was a high crime area, in West Tennessee. White folks didn't go down there unless they were going to buy drugs or were looking for trouble. As he was leaving the building, he passed a bowl of fruit that was sitting on the table and the Lord said, *"Pick up some fruit, take some fruit with you. I'm going to give you some fruit tonight."* So he stuck a tangerine in his pocket. When he arrived at the meeting hall, this young fellow came up to him and said, *"Brother Drake, I got a man you need to talk to; he needs to give his life to the Lord."*

This guy was skinny as a rail, no teeth and all stooped over.

The Lord said, *"Give him the fruit."* Dr. Drake reached into his pocket, pulled out the tangerine and this guy didn't even look up, he just reached out grabbed it, peeled, and devoured it. That night he gave his life to the Lord.

The Lord said *"Ask him what his name is."*

Dr. Drake said, *"What's your name, brother?"*

"They call me Spook."

Dr. Drake *"I didn't ask you what they call you, I said what's your name?"*

"My name is Charles King."

Dr. Drake said, *"You'll forever be Charles King to me. It's Spook no more. You'll never be on the streets again because I'm taking you home with me. God's going to turn your life around."*

What a testimony. Everyone called Charles - Spook for most of his life but before he was buried, in 2004, they called him the Reverend Charles King. He had been the keynote speaker at the Martin Luther King celebration that year. The community now has a Thanksgiving dinner every year in his honor. Charles King! They call me Spook. What enduring fruit God can give us. If we just obey.

How many Charles Kings are in the world? How encouraged would you be to witness to a guy who is strung out on drugs and alcohol and planning to commit murder? Then, God intervenes and turns his life around. Charles King was quite a man; quite a royal man.

The legacy of the town where he lived, a town notoriously full of sin and crime and racism. Charles King didn't like white folks. And God had Dr. Drake team him up with a prayer partner, a white man, named Billy. Billy didn't like black folks, and before they got done praying with each other they were best of friends. And they decided that "We were okay, regardless of our color." What a wonderful thing Jesus can do. When we see these kinds of things, and when I think about what God is going to do with you. And I see what he did with Charles King. And my goodness he's starting with a diamond already. So what is he going to do with you, And in your life?

Joe Rott

God told Dr. Richard Drake to reserve the web domain address *SeminaryOnline.com* and to develop it and post it on the internet on Y2K, January 1, 2000, when many thought the cyber world was going to collapse. He didn't know anything about developing a website; he barely knew how to get online; so he began to pray for God to send him someone who could help. The police showed up at the door of The Good Samaritan Center.

Dr. Drake had been ministering to the least, the last and the lost, to anyone God would send to the Center. The police had with them a young, red headed, freckle faced kid, by the name of Joe Rott. They had found him sleeping on top of one of the old buildings down town. Well, God had heard their prayers, both of them.

Dr. Drake was praying in desperation for God to send him someone to help develop an internet presence for *Seminary Online*. Joe Rott, who was cold, hungry and homeless, on top of a filthy, lonely roof top, was praying for God to help him. Joe Rott's father was in the computer business and Joe was a computer whiz. Together, Dr. Drake and he developed the first internet presence for the SeminaryOnline.com website and posted it online Y2K, January 1, 2000.

What an awesome God we serve. God will never give you a vision without also giving you the provision.

Early in 2002, in Dr. Drake's second year in Phoenix, God once again gave him the opportunities to minister to the needs of young men, broken by life's disappointments, hardships and challenges. He had just finished the first "CEO and Leadership" workshop with Dr. Dean Radtke. The University was off to a great start. When, God started sending people in desperate need of constant attention in order to turn their lives around. *"Jobs 4 Jesus"* was developed to transition men from the street to skilled laborers with a heart for Jesus.

Joe Rott and Carlos Rodriguez, two of his boys from Tennessee, were sent for to come and work with this new team.

Once again Dr. Drake started teaching basic Bible knowledge to familiarize these men with the love of God and God's intended purpose and requirements for their lives and how they were to live and respond to others. His fundamental teachings, which went against their normal response, included:

1. Matthew 5:44 *But I say unto you, Love your enemies, bless them that curse you, do good to them that hate you, and pray for them which despitefully use you, and persecute you;*

2. 2 Chronicles 15:7 *Be strong, therefore, and let not your hands be weak and slack, for your work shall be rewarded.*

3. 1 Thessalonians 4 1-12

a. *...Walk so as to please and gratify God ..that you should be separated and set apart for pure and holy living*

b. *...you should abstain and shrink from all sexual vice, 4 That each one of you should know how to possess (control, manage) his own body in consecration, purity, separated from things profane..*

c. *That no man transgress and overreach his brother and defraud him in this matter or defraud his brother in business. For God has not called us to impurity but to consecration*

d. *To make it your ambition and definitely endeavor to live quietly and peacefully, to mind your own affairs, and to work with your hands... So that you may bear yourselves becomingly and be correct and honorable and command the respect of the outside world,*

e. *Being dependent on nobody [self-supporting] and having need of nothing.*

Dr. Drake was also very outspoken on Biblical issues, and fearlessly defended God's word on issues too often nowadays dismissed because of the world's insistence on "political correctness" which waters down the Scripture and undermines the principles set forth in the Gospel.

Leviticus 19:33-35 *And if a stranger sojourn with thee in your land, ye shall not vex him. But the stranger that dwelleth with you shall be unto you as one born among you, and thou shalt love him as thyself; for ye were strangers in the land of Egypt: I am the LORD your God.*

Leviticus 24:22 *You shall have the same law for the sojourner among you as for one of your own nationality, for I am the Lord your God.*

Proverbs 6:16-19 *These six things the Lord hates, indeed, seven are an abomination to Him:*

1. A proud look [the spirit that makes one overestimate himself and underestimate others]

2. A lying tongue

3. Hands that shed innocent blood

4. A heart that manufactures wicked thoughts and plans

5. Feet that are swift in running to evil

6. A false witness who breathes out lies [even under oath]

7. He who sows discord among his brethren.

Abortion Is An Act of Murder

In reference to pregnant women, the term "with child" occurs twenty-six times in the Bible.

In Luke Chapter 1, verses 36 and 41, we are told that Elisabeth conceived a "son" and that the "babe" leaped in her womb. God does not say that a "fetus" leaped in her womb! He says THE BABE leaped. This is the exact same word that God uses to describe Christ in the manger AFTER He is born (Luke 2:12, 16). In God's eyes, an unborn babe and a newborn babe are the same. They are both living human beings!

Please consider Job 3:16 *Or as an hidden untimely birth I had not been; as infants which never saw light.* Job referred to unborn children as INFANTS. Not fetuses! Not masses of tissue! INFANTS! In God's eyes, an unborn child is a living human baby. God never says once that an unborn child is anything less than a human being.

David said in Psalm 51:5 *Behold, I was shapen in iniquity, and in sin did my mother conceive me.* He did not say that a fetus was shapen in iniquity and conceived in iniquity. David, speaking under the inspiration of the Holy Spirit, said that HE was conceived. David, not a blob of tissue, was conceived.

The same is the case in Psalm 139:13-16 *For thou hast possessed my reins: thou hast covered me in my mother's womb. I will praise thee; for I am fearfully and wonderfully made: marvellous are thy works; and that my soul knoweth right well. My substance was not hid from thee, when I was made in secret, and curiously wrought in the lowest parts of the earth. Thine eyes did see my substance, yet being unperfect; and in thy book all my members were written, which in continuance were fashioned, when as yet there was none of them.*

David was in the womb! A literal and living person. The Bible never uses anything less than human terms to describe the unborn.

Notice that in Jeremiah 1:5 we are told that God KNEW Jeremiah: *"Before I formed thee in the belly I knew thee; and before thou camest forth out of the womb I sanctified thee, and I ordained thee a prophet unto the nations."*

To further confirm the fact that God views the unborn child as a person, please consider Exodus 21:22-23 *If men strive, and hurt a woman with child, so that her fruit depart from her, and yet no mischief follow: he shall be surely punished, according as the woman's husband will lay upon him; and he shall pay as the judges determine. And if any mischief follow, then thou shalt give life for life.*

If the woman has a premature birth and the child lives (*"no mischief follows"*), then there's no death penalty. However, if the child dies (or the woman dies) God says the death penalty applies: *"Thou shalt give life for life."* Why would God require the death penalty if He didn't consider the unborn child to be a human being?

God says that life begins at conception, and the unborn child is a human being.

The Bible isn't alone in declaring this truth. Science also declares that an unborn child is just as much an independent human being as you and I are. The original human cell consists of 46 chromosomes, 23 from each parent. At no point during pregnancy does the mother contribute any new cells to the child. The original cell divides itself and multiplies to provide development and growth for the child. Scientifically speaking, the child is just as independent at six months before birth as he will be six months after birth. Yes, the mother does provide nourishment to the unborn child, but she also provides nourishment to the *newborn* child!

At two weeks pregnancy, the "fetus" can move alone. By four weeks the child has limbs, muscle tissue, a heart and heartbeat. Ears, eyes, and small hands are visible by the fifth week. The child responds to touch sensations by the sixth or seventh week. At eight weeks, the baby sometimes tries to take a breath when removed from the mother. At twelve weeks, the child will often struggle for life two or three hours when removed from the mother.

Abortion Involves the Shedding of Innocent Blood

Proverbs 6:16-17 says that God HATES those who shed innocent blood! Deuteronomy 27:25 says, *"Cursed be he that taketh reward to slay an innocent person. And all the people shall say, Amen."* Who could possibly be more innocent than an unborn baby?! Yet, our society has become so wicked that it condones the slaying of 1.5 million innocent children every year. The Bible says that God HATES people who do this. Abortion is wrong because abortion is MURDER!

What the Bible says about homosexuality

The Bible consistently tells us that homosexual activity is a sin:

Genesis 19:1-13 The story of Sodom and Gomorrah

Leviticus 18:22 *Thou shalt not lie with mankind, as with womankind: it is abomination.*

Leviticus 20;13 *If a man also lie with mankind, as he lieth with a woman, both of them have committed an abomination: they shall surely be put to death; their blood shall be upon them.*

Romans 1:26-27 *For this cause God gave them up unto vile affections: for even their women did change the natural use into that which is against nature: And likewise also the men, leaving the natural use of the woman, burned in their lust one toward another; men with men working that which is unseemly, and receiving in themselves that recompence of their error which was meet.*

1 Corinthians 6:9 *Know ye not that the unrighteous shall not inherit the kingdom of God? Be not deceived: neither fornicators, nor idolaters, nor adulterers, nor effeminate, nor abusers of themselves with mankind.*

God does not create a person with homosexual desires. The Bible tells us that people become homosexuals because of sin and ultimately because of their own choice. A person may be born with a greater susceptibility to homosexuality, just as some people are born with a tendency to violence and other sins. That does not excuse the person's choosing to sin by giving in to sinful desires. If a person is born with a greater susceptibility to anger/rage, does that make it right for him to give into those desires? Of course not! The same is true with homosexuality.

Romans 1:24-25 *Wherefore God also gave them up to uncleanness through the lusts of their own hearts, to dishonour their own bodies between themselves: Who changed the truth of God into a lie, and worshipped and served the creature more than the Creator, who is blessed forever. Amen.*

However, the Bible does not describe homosexuality as a "greater" sin than any other. All sin is offensive to God. Homosexuality is just one of the many things listed that will keep a person from the kingdom of God. *"Know ye not that the unrighteous shall not inherit the kingdom of God? Be not deceived: neither fornicators, nor idolaters, nor adulterers, nor effeminate, nor abusers of themselves with mankind, 10 Nor thieves, nor covetous, nor drunkards, nor revilers, nor extortioners, shall inherit the kingdom of God."* 1 Corintians 6:9.

According to the Bible, God's forgiveness is just as available to a homosexual as it is to an adulterer, idol worshipper, murderer, thief, etc. I Corinthians 6:11 *And such were some of you: but ye are washed, but ye are sanctified, but ye are justified in the name of the Lord Jesus, and by the Spirit of our God.*

2 Corinthians 5:17 *Therefore if any man be in Christ, he is a new creature: old things are passed away; behold, all things are become new.*

God also promises the strength for victory over sin, including homosexuality, to all those who will believe in Jesus Christ for their salvation.

Philippians 4:13 *I can do all things through Christ which strengtheneth me.*

Men are without excuse

Romans 1: 19 *For that which is known about God is evident to them and made plain in their inner consciousness, because God [Himself] has shown it to them.*
20 For ever since the creation of the world His invisible nature and attributes, that is, His eternal power and divinity, have been made intelligible and clearly discernible in and through the things that have been made (His handiworks). So [men] are without excuse [altogether without any defense or justification],
21 Because when they knew and recognized Him as God, they did not honor and glorify Him as God or

give Him thanks. But instead they became futile and godless in their thinking [with vain imaginings, foolish reasoning, and stupid speculations] and their senseless minds were darkened.

22 Claiming to be wise, they became fools [professing to be smart, they made simpletons of themselves].

23 And by them the glory and majesty and excellence of the immortal God were exchanged for and represented by images, resembling mortal man and birds and beasts and reptiles.

24 Therefore God gave them up in the lusts of their [own] hearts to sexual impurity, to the dishonoring of their bodies among themselves [abandoning them to the degrading power of sin],

25 Because they exchanged the truth of God for a lie and worshiped and served the creature rather than the Creator, Who is blessed forever! Amen (so be it).

26 For this reason God gave them over and abandoned them to vile affections and degrading passions. For their women exchanged their natural function for an unnatural and abnormal one,

27 And the men also turned from natural relations with women and were set ablaze (burning out, consumed) with lust for one another—men committing shameful acts with men and suffering in their own bodies and personalities the inevitable consequences and penalty of their wrong-doing and going astray, which was [their] fitting retribution.

28 And so, since they did not see fit to acknowledge God or approve of Him or consider Him worth the knowing, God gave them over to a base and condemned mind to do things not proper or decent but loathsome,

29 Until they were filled (permeated and saturated) with every kind of unrighteousness, iniquity, grasping and covetous greed, and malice. [They were] full of envy and jealousy, murder, strife, deceit and treachery, ill will and cruel ways. [They were] secret backbiters and gossipers,

30 Slanderers, hateful to and hating God, full of insolence, arrogance, [and] boasting; inventors of new forms of evil, disobedient and undutiful to parents.

31 [They were] without understanding, conscienceless and faithless, heartless and loveless [and] merciless.

32 Though they are fully aware of God's righteous decree that those who do such things deserve to die, they not only do them themselves but approve and applaud others who practice them.

What the Bible says about a masculine God

What I write is what I have heard said dozens of times, by trusted Bible authorities. My prayer is that the Lord has directed me to thoroughly investigate this topic and substantially plead His case for remaining true to the Written Word; that through the following evidence hearts will be convicted. As Christians, and especially as Christian teachers, authors and educator we should not concern ourselves with anything but what God thinks.

"The masculine/feminine God" is a very sensitive subject; I know of no other alliances that would contemplate entertaining the feminine reference. In fact all staunchly refute the idea of an endorsement to a feminine God. The Holy Spirit imparted a serious catch in my spirit when our Almighty God was referred to in the feminine context. The Bible is clear that God is spirit (John 4:24), and as such, he is not gendered. When we call him father we do not mean that he is male, like human fathers are. Rather, we mean that he relates to us....provides for, protects, leads, and even disciplines us like the best human fathers do, only better (Matthew 6:25-30, 6:7-11, James, Hebrews 12:7-10). Likewise, when the Bible speaks of God as a husband, it does not claim that God is male, but that God jealously guards his relationship with his people like a good husband loves and protects his wife [and family]. Hosea 2:16. [1] The Bible often references God as having attributes which both men and women image uniquely.[2]

If we seek to follow biblical inclusivity, let us also affirm the consistent witness of the church, namely, that God is neither feminine nor masculine (gender), neither male nor female (sex). God, who is transcendent Spirit, possesses no physical body, yet accommodates to human limitations by using physical, relational, gender-laden images for self-disclosure.[3]

As a Theological University, we are expected to have straight answers, to know Biblical Truths and to be firm in our faith and commitment to teach only what is the acceptable will of the Lord; good, pleasing and perfect in God's sight. The Church needs no more separation over petty arguments or issues that are of no eternal consequence.

Although there are numerous references in the Bible to the Mothering, Nurturing and the Gentleness of God's love; NEVER IS GOD REFERRED TO IN THE FEMININE TENSE. We are not here to rewrite the inspired Word of God; believing, that if God wanted to be viewed in the feminine, He would have addressed Himself in such a manner somewhere in the 66 books of the **God-breathed** inspiration Word/Bible.

Jesus regularly addressed God as "Father." Jesus often called God…Abba and encouraged his followers to do the same. Abba means "daddy" or "papa"… a term of intimacy and nurturance… God cannot be limited to a single category. Jesus shifted the parental image… to the picture of a god who nourishes and guides, a god who could be called "Papa."[4]

Genesis 1:27 *So God created man in his own image, in the image of God he created him; male and female he created them.*

Galatians 3:28 *In Christ there is no Jew or Greek, slave or citizen, male or female. All are one in Christ Jesus.*

2 Timothy 3:16 (KJV) *All scripture is given by inspiration of God, and is profitable for doctrine, for reproof, for correction, for instruction in righteousness.*

Matthew5:18 (KJV) *For verily I say unto you, Till heaven and earth pass, one jot or one tittle shall in no wise pass… till all be fulfilled.*

The quotation uses "jot and title" as an example of extremely minor details. The phrase "jot and tittle" indicates that every small detail has received attention.[5]

Proverbs 30:5-7 (NIV) *Every word of God is flawless;*

he is a shield to those who take refuge in him. 6 Do not add to his words....

1 Timothy 1: (AMP) 3 *... [do] not teach any different doctrine,...4 Nor... give importance to or occupy themselves ... which foster and promote useless speculations and questionings rather than acceptance in faith of God's administration and the divine training that is in faith.*

The express desire of Phoenix University of Theology International is to unite the body of Christ. We teach what is relevant and give no importance to that which fosters and promote useless speculations and questionings rather than acceptance in faith and has NO eternal consequence.

Using the feminine metaphor for our limitless God, is insidious; it presents in a seemingly harmless way but actually with grave effects that will undermine the strength of the Gospel. Following are two examples of the deceptive reference to God in the feminine. The Gospel warns us in: 1 Corinthians 15:33 (AMP) *Do not be so deceived and misled!*

During his brief pontificate, Pope John Paul I, made this innovative statement: "God is Father, and even more, He is Mother." The assertion was received with surprise in innumerable Catholic circles and with undisguised joy among the more radical progressivists. [6]

An unnamed author stated, "I am not afraid to address God as Mother when I feel vulnerable and as Father when I need guidance and protection. I agree with the wiccan concept of the God."[7]

Ours is not to confuse and confound the world as the secular education systems do. God was called Father or "Abba" by Jesus; As Christians, we have the privilege of also calling God "Abba" Our belief is that if we would reference God in any other manner it would be Biblically inaccurate.

From my reading it appears that much of the need to have God referred to in the feminine context has largely been promoted by those whose own father was too unreliable to provide any positive image of God; or those who have experienced a personal trauma with their parents or spouse.[8]

This, only too often scenario increases the need to emphasize that the Bible is clear that God is spirit (John 4:24), and as such, he is not gendered. Also, that The Bible often references God as having attributes that both men and women image uniquely. Teaching that the Agape love we receive from our Abba is eternal, unconditional and beyond anything we could ever imagine of an earthly figure.

To quicken the Spirit in a person to the realization of the limitless love of God would bring to light any family baggage someone could be carrying around that might be keeping them from having a better relationship with God.[9] Praying this information has dispelled any need to reference God in a distinctly feminine context. Which I continue to believe has no Biblical connotation and boarders on the solicitation of those on the fringe. May the Holy Spirit of the LORD make clear to you through increase in your wisdom, understanding and knowledge the perfect will of God.

1, 2 & 7. God's Feminine Attributes – Blog, Date: July 12, 2011, Author Pastor Eric D. Naus
3, FEMININE IMAGES FOR GOD: WHAT DOES THE BIBLE SAY? by Dr. Margo G. Houts, professor of Religion and Theology
4. Wikipedia the free encyclopedia
5. GOD AS MOTHER, Sunstone, by Carrie A. Miles
6-9. Is God Mother? Background of a Pontifical Statement, Atila Sinke Guimarães

CHAPTER 3

UNDER THE HAND OF GOD

Dr. Richard Drake tells the story of how miraculously during a time of prayer he fell under the power and could not get up from the floor. He said, it was like he was stuck to the floor, some people call it being slain in the spirit. He just knew something put him on the floor and kept him there. Then the Lord began to speak to him, into him, and through him, and He said,

"The mystery is, there is no mystery
I'm as real as the rising sun,
the author of all wisdom,
the source of all power
Fast and pray
Preach Jesus and Him crucified.
All my gifts I give unto you as you have need to do
My will."

What an emboldening and empowering statement. Mystery means something that is to be revealed.

The mystery that there is no mystery says, there's nothing to be revealed that hasn't been revealed in Christ Jesus. If you lack wisdom, then you seek God who is the author of all wisdom. James 1:5 tells us, *"If any of you lacks wisdom, you should ask God, who gives generously to all without finding fault, and it will be given to you."*

The source of all power gives us the confidence that the devil himself has no power that God has not given him and He's given us more than He's given him, so we know that we are more than conquerors. So don't fear what the devil may do to you. because you know he has no right into your life or circumstances, lest you should allow him in by breaking the law or getting outside God's will. Otherwise, I'm ok and you're ok. So if we stay on God's mission and in God's will we always have victory over the enemy.

The Bible tells us in Luke 10:18 *And He (Jesus) said to them, I saw Satan falling like a lightning [flash] from heaven. 19 Behold! I have given you authority and power to trample upon serpents and scorpions, and [physical and mental strength and ability] over all the power that the enemy [possesses]; and nothing shall in any way harm you.*

What a mighty God we serve. We can learn such tremendously exciting things about the awesome presence of the power of God from His Word and how it affects our lives; and then incredible, incredible things happen!

We need to be seeking the truth and power from God by studying His Word. Men should never impress us very much, because we can find men to agree with us on just about anything. Even the church; experience has shown that you can find a church that believes about whatever you want it to. When you give your life to the Lord and surrender to the ministry, you should not look so much for what a man can teach you about what he knows or thinks, but search the Word of God, because you want to know what God's truth is.

The Lord will teach you, and that revelation that comes; we call revelation education, is the most valuable education that we receive, because first of all it comes from the author of all wisdom; it comes from the Lord. It is permanently engrained in our minds, our heart, and our spirits and we can speak it with boldness and without notes; we become one with revelation education. Revelation education includes inspiration and invention. So when we see that men and women are being creative, we know that they have had a revelational-educational-experience. They have a vision for something; unfortunately, the world has ceased giving God the credit for being our teacher.

You will also see in the scripture, that one of the things the Scribes and Pharisees noticed about Jesus was that He had not been formally educated. They said, *"...wherein has this man letters."*

John 7:14-16 **Now about the midst of the feast Jesus went up into the temple, and taught. And the Jews marveled, saying, How knoweth this man letters, having never learned? Jesus answered them, and said, My doctrine is not mine, but His that sent me.**

2 Timothy 3:15-17 tells us, **"The Holy Scriptures, which are able to make you wise for salvation through faith which is in Christ Jesus. All Scripture is given by inspiration of God, and is profitable for doctrine, for reproof, for correction, for instruction in righteous- ness, that the man of God may be complete, thoroughly equipped for every good work."**

What the Scribes and Pharisees were saying is; *"He didn't go to our school. Where did he learn this stuff?"*

He was obviously well studied. He was obviously a learned man. In the scripture it tells us that he was asking 'Doctors of the Law' questions when He was 12 years old. But He was like one who attends Phoenix University of

Theology International. He got his information from His heavenly Father, his Daddy; who taught Him; and then He taught with boldness and authority because His education was revelation education, it was from God!

How excited it is to be instructed by the author of all wisdom, to be empowered by the source of all power, to be granted every gift we need to do His will when we have need to do His will. Isn't it incredible, what a mighty God we serve.

1 Peter 4:10 *As each of you has received a gift (a particular spiritual talent, a gracious divine endowment), employ it for one another as good trustees of God's many-sided grace [faithful stewards of the extremely diverse powers and gifts granted to Christians by unmerited favor].*

CHAPTER 4

THE LORD IS OUR TEACHER

The Scribes and Pharisees said the same of the apostles when they noticed that they were ignorant and unlearned men, they had not been to college. In the same way the world has beat us down to the point that we think if we don't have their piece of paper showing that we stayed in class long enough, paid enough money, to get a piece of paper that testifies that we know something we don't know, it says we can do something we can't do, and yet we're proud of it. And yet those people who possess the words of life, who possess the power for eternal life, who have the strength and solid doctrine and truth often go without any letters or recognition. This has gone on far too long. Why?

Because the church quit doing what it was sanctioned to do; to teach and qualify by providing the necessary skills, knowledge and credentials to produce competent instructors in the Word and then to validate their gifting and ability with documentation or "letters" to confirm and validate their depth of knowledge and understanding of the Word of God and their skills and ability to teach with boldness and confidence.

Phoenix University of Theology International doesn't have a problem with any- one who testifies that Jesus Christ is Lord and has received salvation by faith through grace whether they're Catholic, Baptist, or Pentecostal. 1 John 4:*2 every spirit which acknowledges and confesses that Jesus Christ (the Messiah) [has actually] become man and has come in the flesh, is of God.*

It is not our mission to get people speaking in tongues, tongues is one of the gifts, and not everyone possesses every gift. We're on a mission to get people knowing Jesus, by validating those who can boldly teach sound, consistent doctrine. We are providing students with the credentials they need so they can boldly and confidently go and teach God's Word to multitudes, to change their hearts and minds to Christ.

God will teach us what we need to know. The Lord is our teacher. Many qualified men and women in full time ministry find out that they don't have the time or the money to complete college. That is why Phoenix University of

Theology International is such a critical part of God's work, a revelation, if you will. To provide a way for these gifted and qualified men and women to receive the credentials they deserve because of their self motivated study and revelation education; we do this through the evaluation of their "lifelong learning".

Dr. Richard Drake heard about credit for life experience, CLEP, which stands for, College Level Examination Program. He had been teaching adult Bible school since he was a teenager. He was one of the lecturers for the Presbyterian denomination. He knew The Word. He knew he could do most of what any preacher could do, but there were things that he was lacking. When he went to the Seminary he said to the professors, *"Examine me, see what I need and give it to me and send me, I'm late."*

At that time Theological Schools didn't know how to evaluate prior learning experience and they were concerned that it would affect their accreditation. They didn't know how to give credit for what a person has already learned. Dr. Drake was shocked when the president of the seminary asked him, *"How do you know when you speak in tongues that it's from the Lord and not from the devil?"* Richard reciting from Matthew 7:11 and Luke 11:13 "I read a scripture that says '*If you, then, though you are evil, know how to give good gifts to your children, how much more will your Father in heaven give good gifts to those who ask him!'* We know that God answers our prayers. We've got victory over Satan and **it is the power of the testimony and the witness of the presence of God's wisdom and God's spirit in our lives that validate our credentials**."

We are warned in 2 Timothy 3:1-8 *But know this, that in the last days perilous times will come: men will... 5 have a form of godliness but denying its power... from such people turn away... 7 always learning and never able to come to the knowledge of the truth. 8 so do these also resist the truth: men of corrupt minds, disapproved concerning the faith.*

1 Timothy 1:6-7 also tells us, *"6 But certain individuals have missed the mark .... [and] have wandered away into vain arguments and discussions and purposeless talk.*

7 They have no understanding either of the words and terms they use or of the subjects about which they make dogmatic assertions. Thereby, they are undermining the faith of some."

The majority of ministers in the world have degrees or graduate degrees. A hundred percent of them in some of the mainline denominations have degrees because they are required before ordination. The denominations that have the fewest number of ministers with graduate degrees are Independent and Pentecostal; only 17 to 20 percent. However, they are neither ignorant nor unlearned. They are burning the world up for Jesus. Their ministries are growing faster than the mainline denominations because they've been studying the Word of God and learning from God, receiving revelation education.

So many times we find ourselves frightened because we think we are going to fail God. But, what an exciting time it is when God empowers us. So, what we're doing at Phoenix University of Theology International is confirming, the best way we can what you've learned from your Heavenly Father about His Word and His doctrine. Then we're going to validate what you've learned with the degree that you receive. In the process we're going to prepare you with those things that we feel, jointly, mutually, you and the university; feel you need, to equip yourself, to properly prepare yourself to present Christ in truth and power to a lost and dying world. So you'll go out with the letter that says, Doctor. And you know what's going to back that letter up? Not our signatures, but **your gift, your faith, your presence, and your presentation of God's call and purpose in your life. Amen.**

CHAPTER 5

REVELATION REVEALED

Dr. Richard Drake said that God would ask him questions? One of the questions was,"*What cup did Jesus drink out of at the Passover?*" He began to research and discovered in the writings of Martin Luther who said, "*The languages are the sheath in which the sword of the spirit is contained, and sometimes a little word can make such a big difference in what we understand is being said.*" In the original Scripture it says that on that night Jesus took "*the*" cup. When we read a revised Bible today it most likely will say on that night Jesus took "a" cup.

Well he did not take a cup; he took "*the*" cup. The cup of God's wrath, from which every nation shall drink, you'll find this in Psalm 75:8 ***For in the hand of the LORD there is <u>the</u> cup, and the wine is red; it is full of mixture; and he poureth out of the same: but the dregs thereof, all the***

wicked of the earth shall wring them out, and drink them.
Jesus took *"the"* cup, which was on the table as the Elijah cup to announce the messiah.

Even today when the Jews fill the Elijah cup they say as they pour the wine into the cup, *"God pour out your wrath."* So Jesus took that cup and He blessed it, and so the cup that is death and judgment to the rest of the world is life and health and healing to the rest of us. Jesus drank the dregs, so now there is healing and there is life and there is power and there is salvation in the cup. Everything we needed is in the cup, when we drink it by faith, because He drank the dregs on our behalf. It is between you and Jesus when you come and by faith take the cup.

Jewish Tradition

The Jews drink four cups of wine at the Seder meal. The four cups of wine correspond to the four promises or expressions of redemption made by God to the Israelites in Exodus 6:2

2 God said to Moses, "I am the LORD. 3 I appeared to Abraham, to Isaac and to Jacob as God Almighty, but by my name the LORD I did not make myself fully known to them. 4 I also established my covenant with them to give them the land of Canaan, where

82

they resided as foreigners. 5 Moreover, I have heard the groaning of the Israelites, whom the Egyptians are enslaving, and I have remembered my covenant.

6 "Therefore, say to the Israelites:

1. I am the LORD, and I will bring you out from under the yoke of the Egyptians. – 'Vehotzeiti'

2. I will free you from being slaves to them, 'Vehitzalti' and

3. I will redeem you with an outstretched arm and with mighty acts of judgment. – 'Vega'alti'

4. 7 I will take you as my own people, and I will be your God.

Then you will know that I am the LORD your God, who brought you out from under the yoke of the Egyptians. – 'Velakachti'."

The Jewish people did not go from a slave nation to being the Chosen People at Mount Sinai overnight. There were different stages of redemption. The above phrases described these different stages. Each cup of wine represents one of these levels.

The Seder dinner not only commemorates the historical redemption from Egyptian bondage of the Jewish people but also calls to mind their future redemption when Elijah and the Messiah shall appear.

On the night when they celebrate their redemption from Egypt, they also express their absolute belief in the coming of the Messiah, the one who will lead them out of this exile and take them all back to their land. They are so confident of their imminent redemption, that they actually pour a cup of wine for Elijah, the prophet who will come to announce the arrival of the Messiah.

There is a fifth expression of redemption that follows immediately afterward: Exodus 6:8 *And I will bring you to the land I swore with uplifted hand to give to Abraham, to Isaac and to Jacob. I will give it to you as a possession. I am the LORD. - "Veheveiti."*

This is seen as a reference to the future redemption, to be announced by Elijah the Prophet, when God will gather the Jews from the "four corners of the earth" and return them to their Land. This level of redemption is represented by the fifth cup, called "Elijah's Cup," which is poured but not drank.

The Jewish people believe that the five expressions of freedom are various stages in the redemption process. The first four are stages that they work on and achieve—the fifth, the final redemption is something that God will fulfill. They believe they must do everything that leads up to it, but the final step has to be taken by God. That is why they do not drink the Cup of Elijah.

The Jewish tradition of wrapping and hiding the middle piece of motza, or the Afikomen, which is our communion bread, represents a depiction of the events of Christ's betrayal, death and resurrection.

Luke 22:19 *And he took bread, gave thanks and broke it, and gave it to them, saying, "This is my body given for you; do this in remembrance of me."* Jesus the Messiah would have taken the middle one of the three pieces of motza, the piece that stood for the priest or mediator between God and the people, He broke it as His body would be broken, wrapped half in a linen napkin as he would be wrapped in linen, for burial, hidden it as he would be buried, brought it back as he would be resurrected, and distributed it to everyone seated with him, as He would distribute His life to all who believe. As He did this, he was conscious that this middle piece of motza represented His own, spotless body given for the redemption of His people. As the motza is striped and pierced, His own body would be striped and pierced, and it is by those wounds that we are healed

Isaiah 53: 5 *But he was pierced for our transgressions, he was crushed for our iniquities; the punishment that brought us peace was on him, and by his wounds we are healed.*

The Jewish people do not recognize Jesus as the Messiah or John the Baptist as Elijah as spoken of in these references, John 1: 29 *Behold, the Lamb of God who takes away the sin of the world!* Matthew 17:11-13 *He replied, Elijah does come and will get everything restored and ready, 12 But I tell you that Elijah has come already, and they did not know or recognize him, but did to him as they liked. So also the Son of Man is going to be treated and suffer at their hands. 13 Then the disciples understood that He spoke to them about John the Baptist.*

Mark 9:12-13 **Jesus replied,** *"To be sure, Elijah does come first, and restores all things. Why then is it written that the Son of Man must suffer much and be rejected? 13 But I tell you, Elijah has come, and they have done to him everything they wished, just as it is written about him."*

CHAPTER 6

3 Days and 3 Nights - The Sign of Jonah

We know that Jonah was in the belly of the fish for three days and three nights, it tells us that in, Jonah 1:16-17 *Then the men feared the LORD exceedingly, and offered a sacrifice unto the LORD, and made vows. Now the LORD had prepared a great fish to swallow up Jonah.* *And Jonah was in the belly of the fish three days and three nights.*

Now, we also know that between Friday afternoon, when Jesus died on the Cross and Sunday morning, when He was risen from the dead, is not three (3) days and three (3) nights. Jesus died on that cross, about the ninth hour, on Friday afternoon, only hours from the Sabbath Day, which is Saturday, when the law required that no work should be done.

What Jesus was telling the disciples, In Matthew 12:40 when He said, *"So will the son of Man be three days and three nights in the heart of the earth, "* was that God would remove the protective angels that the Bible speaks of in, Luke 4:10-12 *For it is written, He shall give his angels charge over thee, to keep thee. 11 And in their hands they shall bear thee up, lest at any time thou dash thy foot against a stone.* The word **heart** in Hebrew, is kar-dee'ah or in Latin, cor, which denotes the centre of all physical and spiritual life, the soul or mind, as it is the fountain and seat of the thoughts, our will and character.

Therefore, on the evening of Passover, after partaking of the meal, when Jesus took *"the"* cup, which was the Elijah cup; it was on the table to announce the Messiah. He drank *the cup of God's wrath,* from which every nation shall drink, you'll find this in Psalm 75:8 *For in the hand of the LORD there is the cup, and the wine is red; it is full of mixture;… the dregs thereof, all the wicked of the earth shall wring them out, and drink them.*

From the moment that Jesus drank the dregs, He was cast into *the heart of the earth.* He was in the "cor" "kardia" heart of the earth, the centre of all physical and spiritual life, with all of its evil will and deceitful character. We know this because in Luke it tells us that *"the angels would bear Him up, lest at any time He would dash His foot against a stone.* " But, from the moment he "drank from *the cup of God's wrath*", he was vulnerable, susceptible to being seized, wounded, open to physical attack and crucifixion.

How else, could He have been betrayed? As depicted in Matthew 26:67 *Then they spit in his face and struck him with their fists. Others slapped him,* and in Matthew 27 26 *Then the governor's soldiers took Jesus into the Praet rium and gathered the whole company of soldiers around him. 28 They stripped him and put a scarlet robe on him, 29 and then twisted together a crown of thorns and set it on his head. They put a staff in his right hand... 30 They spit on him, and took the staff and struck him on the head again and again. 31 After they had mocked him... Then they led him away to crucify him.*

So, from Thursday evening, Jesus was in the kardia of the earth, which is full of sin and pain and hatred. He like you and me felt every slap, every fist and every ounce of pain, humility and defeat that we would have felt going through those treacherous hours of degradation and disgrace. No wonder He cried out as stated in Mark 15:34 *My God, My God, why have You forsaken Me?* Then, after He breathed His last, he was plunged into the realm or dominion of satan, where He had conquest over sin and death.

Therefore, the three nights, are from the time He drank from the Elijah cup, Thursday night, Friday night and Saturday night and the three days were Friday; the day He was crucified and died on the cross, Saturday, and then on Sunday, the third day, He rose again.

This was to fulfill what was spoken through the prophet Isaiah: *"He took up our infirmities and bore our diseases."* Matthew 8:17 and in Isaiah 53:4 *Surely he took up our pain and bore our suffering, 5 But he was pierced for our transgressions, he was crushed for our iniquities; the punishment that brought us peace was on him, and by his wounds we are healed. 6We all, like sheep, have gone astray, each of us has turned to our own way; and the LORD has laid on him the iniquity of us all. 7 he was led like a lamb to the slaughter, 8 for he was cut off from the land of the living; for the transgression of my people he was punished. 9 He was assigned a grave with the wicked, and with the rich in his death, 10 the LORD makes his life an offering for sin, 11 After he has suffered, he will see the light of life and be satisfied by his knowledge my righteous servant will justify many, and he will bear their iniquities. 12 He poured out his life unto death, and was numbered with the transgressors. He bore the sin of many, and made intercession for the transgressors.*

Scripture reference to the sign of Jonah

1. Luke 11:30 *For as Jonah became a sign to the people of Nineveh, so will also the Son of Man be to this age and generation.*

2. Matthew 12:38-39 *Then some of the scribes and Pharisees said to Him, Teacher, we desire to see a sign or miracle from you. But He replied to them, an evil and adulterous generation seeks and demands a sign; but no sign shall be given to it except the sign of the prophet Jonah.*

3. Matthew 16:4 *A wicked and morally unfaithful generation craves a sign, but no sign shall be given to it except the sign of the prophet Jonah. Then He left them and went...*

4. Luke 11:29 *Now as the crowds were thronging Him, He began to say, This present generation is a wicked one; it seeks and demands a sign, but no sign shall be given to it except the sign of Jonah.*

Scripture reference to the time of Jesus Death:

Matthew 27:45 *Now from the sixth hour there was darkness over all the land unto the ninth hour. 46 And about the ninth hour Jesus cried with a loud voice, saying, "Eli, Eli, lama sabachthani?" That is to say, "My God, my God, why hast thou forsaken me?"... 50 Jesus, when he had cried again with a loud voice, yielded up the ghost.*

Scripture reference to the day and events of the Last Supper:

Matthew 26:17 *On the first day of the Festival of Unleavened Bread, the disciples came to Jesus and asked, "Where do you want us to make preparations for you to eat the Passover?"... 26 While they were eating, Jesus took bread, and when he had given thanks, he broke it and gave it to his disciples, saying, "Take and eat; this is my body."*

Matthew 26: 27 *Then he took a cup, and when he had given thanks, he gave it to them, saying, "Drink from it, all of you. 28 This is my blood of the covenant, which is poured out for many for the forgiveness of sins."*

Jesus took "the" cup, which was the Elijah cup, it was on the table to announce the messiah. He took "the" cup of

God's wrath, from which every nation shall drink, you'll find this in Psalm 75: 8 *For in the hand of the LORD there is the cup, and the wine is red; it is full of mixture; ... the dregs thereof, all the wicked of the earth shall wring them out, and drink them.*

Scripture reference to God's protective angels over Jesus life:

Matthew 4:5-7 *Then the devil taketh him up into the holy city, and setteth him on a pinnacle of the temple, 6 And saith unto him, "If thou be the Son of God, cast thyself down: for it is written, He shall give his angels charge concerning thee: and in their hands they shall bear thee up, lest at any time thou dash thy foot against a stone."*

This is also, in Luke 4:10-12 *For it is written, "He shall give his angels charge over thee, to keep thee... 11And in their hands they shall bear thee up, lest at any time thou dash thy foot against a stone."*

And again in Psalms 91:11-13 *For he shall give his angels charge over thee, to keep thee in all thy ways. 12They shall bear thee up in their hands, lest thou dash thy foot against a stone. 13Thou shalt tread upon the lion and adder: the young lion and the dragon shalt thou trample under feet.*

Scripture reference to the events leading up to Jesus crucifixion, death and resurrection:

Matthew26: 36 *Then Jesus went with his disciples to a place called Gethsemane, and he said to them, "Sit here while I go over there and pray." 37 He took Peter and the two sons of Zebedee along with him, and he began to be sorrowful and troubled. 38 Then he said to them, "My soul is overwhelmed with sorrow to the point of death. Stay here and keep watch with me."*

Then in Mark 14:43 *And at once, while He was still speaking, Judas came, one of the Twelve [apostles], and with him a crowd of men with swords and clubs, [who came] from the chief priests and the scribes and the elders [of the Sanhedrin]. 44 Now the betrayer had given them a signal, saying, "The One I shall kiss is [the Man]; seize Him and lead [Him] away safely [so as to prevent His escape]." 45 And when he came, he went up to Jesus immediately and said, "Master! Master!" and he embraced Him and kissed Him fervently. 46 And they threw their hands on Him and arrested Him.*

Later in Matthew 26, it tells us in verse 67 *Then they spit in his face and struck him with their fists. Others slapped him.*

Matthew 27:27 *Then the governor's soldiers took Jesus into the Praetorium and gathered the whole company of soldiers around him. 28 They stripped him and put a scarlet robe on him, 29 and then twisted together a crown of thorns and set it on his head. They put a staff in his right hand... 30 They spit on him, and took the staff and struck him on the head again and again. 31 After they had mocked him... Then they led him away to crucify him.*

On that Friday He was allowed to die upon the cross. Matthew 27:57 *As evening approached, there came a rich man from Arimathea, named Joseph, who had himself become a disciple of Jesus. 58 Going to Pilate, he asked for Jesus' body, and Pilate ordered that it be given to him. 59 Joseph took the body, wrapped it in a clean linen cloth, 60 and placed it in his own new tomb that he had cut out of the rock. He rolled a big stone in front of the entrance to the tomb and went away.*

Matthew 28:1 *After the Sabbath, at dawn on the first day of the week, Mary Magdalene and the other Mary went to look at the tomb... 5 The angel said to the women, "Do not be afraid, for I know that you are looking for Jesus, who was crucified 6 He is not here, he has risen, just as he said."*

CHAPTER 7

THE BRIDE OF CHRIST
- THE CHURCH

What came out of Jesus when he gave up the ghost?
Woman, the church! Out of the second Adam, from his
side, from his wounded, pierced side, having received the
spirit of life and purity and holiness and righteousness into
the kingdom, God began to reconstruct or to build; like it
says in Genesis 2, God *"builded Adam a woman"*, Darby
Translation, Genesis 2: *21 And Jehovah Elohim caused a*
deep sleep to fall upon Man; and he slept. And he took
one of his ribs and closed up flesh in its stead. 22And
Jehovah Elohim built the rib that he had taken from Man
into a woman; and brought her to Man. 23And Man said,
"This time it is bone of my bones and flesh of my flesh:
this shall be called Woman, because this was taken out
of a man."

God began to build Christ a bride and you and I are single cells in that living eternal righteous glorious holy life. We are being reborn collectively as a woman, pure and righteous, the bride of Christ. In just one question God can get your mind and heart and theology and doctrine all engaged in a revelation that will change your life. Now, we can begin to understand why the church is referred to as the bride. We are betrothed to Christ. The "*Bride*" is the body of believers that comprise the universal Christian Ekklesia (Church literally "called-out ones").

In Ephesians 5, wives are compared to the assembly: *22 Wives, [submit yourselves] to your own husbands, as to the Lord, 23 for a husband is head of the wife, as also the Christ [is] head of the assembly. *He* [is] Saviour of the body. 24 But even as the assembly is subjected to the Christ, so also wives to their own husbands in everything. 25 Husbands, love your own wives, even as the Christ also loved the assembly, and has delivered himself up for it, 26 in order that he might sanctify it, purifying [it] by the washing of water by [the] word, 27 that *he* might present the assembly to himself glorious, having no spot, or wrinkle, or any of such things; but that it might be holy and blameless. 28 So ought men also to love their* *own wives as their own bodies: he that loves his own wife loves himself. 29 For no one has ever hated his own flesh, but nourishes and cherishes it, even as also the Christ the assembly: 30 for we are members of his body; [we are of his flesh, and of his bones.]*

In the oldest translations assembly referred to a being or an entity it is the feminine past participle of assembler.

CHAPTER 8

FIRST BORN OF THE DEAD

Jesus was the first born of the dead. Matthew 27:50 *Jesus, when he had cried again with a loud voice, yielded up the ghost. 51And, behold, the veil of the temple was rent in twain from the top to the bottom; and the earth did quake, and the rocks rent; 52And the graves were opened; and many bodies of the saints which slept arose, 53And came out of the graves <u>after his resurrection, and went into the holy city, and appeared unto many.</u>*

<u>I will draw all "Judgment" unto myself</u>

God can teach you so much with a question. Then He will send you in search for the answer and when you've dug hard enough and long enough, He'll give you the answer simply enough that you will have the information to write a book that can change a generation of people and lives.

You know the scripture where Jesus said now judgment is come? The time for judgment is come?

John 12: 31 *Now is the judgment of this world: now shall the prince of this world be cast out. 32 And, if I be lifted up from the earth, will draw all* **men** *unto me.* In modern translations, the word "men" is italicized which means that the translators put that in there for emphasis. But, if you remember diagramming sentences in English class like I do, you know that the subject of that sentence is not men it is judgment. Jesus was actually saying, *"and if I be lifted up I will draw all judgment unto me."*

Isn't that what Jesus actually did? Because he took upon himself all judgment, because he drank from the cup, you and I can go to him for forgiveness. You see, All men are not drawn to the Lord we know that by experience and by the word.

CHAPTER 9

CHRIST IN YOU THE HOPE OF GLORY

As Christ Jesus had been the master, <u>counselor</u> and guide to believers, He promised to send the Holy Spirit as His substitute so that He might abide with us forever, John 14:16 *And I will ask the Father, and he will give you another advocate to help you and be with you forever.*

In believers' lives, the Holy Spirit has full, immediate, and universal influence, as the Scripture so wonderfully teaches in II Corinthians 3:17-18 *Now the Lord is the Spirit, and where the Spirit of the Lord is, there is liberty (emancipation from bondage, freedom). And all of us, as with unveiled face, [because we] continued to behold [in the Word of God] as in a mirror the glory of the Lord, are constantly being transfigured into His very own image in ever increasing splendor and from one degree of glory to another (from glory to glory); [for this comes] from the Lord [Who is] the Spirit.*

Colossians 1:26-28 *The mystery of which was hidden for ages and generations from angels and men], but is now revealed to His holy people (the saints), 27 To whom God was pleased to make known how great for the Gentiles are the riches of the glory of this mystery, which is Christ within and among you, the Hope of [realizing the] glory.*

Ephesians 1:13 *In Him you also who have heard the Word of Truth, the glad tidings (Gospel) of your salvation, and have believed in and adhered to and relied on Him, were stamped with the seal of the long-promised Holy Spirit.*

Ephesians 1:18 *I pray also that the eyes of your heart may be enlightened in order that you may know the hope to which he has called you, the riches of his glorious inheritance in the saints.*

What the eye is to the body, that is the mind to the soul; God, wants our "hearts" to be right, He also wants our "understanding" to be right. Our understanding has been blinded by sin; however, studying the Word of God enlightens the mind by understanding. So, we may shed light on the intellect of the world, and restore the weak and perverted mind to a just view of the proportion of things, and to the true knowledge of God, fully comprehending the great truths which pertain to the divine administration.

Romans 5:1-3 *Therefore, since we are justified (acquitted, declared righteous, and given a right standing with God) through faith, let us [grasp the fact that we] have [the peace of reconciliation to hold and to enjoy] peace with God through our Lord Jesus Christ (the Messiah, the Anointed One). 2 Through Him also we have [our] access (entrance, introduction) by faith into this grace (state of God's favor) in which we [firmly and safely] stand. And let us rejoice and exult in our hope of experiencing and enjoying the glory of God. 3 Moreover [let us also be full of joy now!] let us exult and triumph in our troubles and rejoice in our sufferings, knowing that pressure and affliction and hardship produce patient and unswerving endurance.*

To purchase additional copies of this book, or to contact Dr. Karen E. Drake for speaking engagements, contact:

Phoenix University of Theology International

Box 86054

Phoenix, AZ 85080

email: PhoenixUTI@gmail.com

Proof

Made in the USA
Charleston, SC
08 September 2015